A Free Gift

I want to say Thank You for buying my book so I put together a free gift for you!

Nutrients and Smart Drugs That Help Memory

This gift is the perfect complement to this book so just visit the link below to get access.

http://www.mylanderpages.com/freegifts/MentalMastery

Thanks!

Jason

Table of Contents

Introduction

We all have a general idea of what a memory actually is. It's when you can recall a special event. It's when you can recall going out on your first date. From a scientific standpoint, memory is a set or processes that our brain goes through in order to receive, store, keep, and recall information. With memory, there are three major processes.

The first major process is encoding. This means that our brain takes the information it receives and processes it in a form that is usable. The second major process is storage. Many of our memories are actually stored on the outside of our awareness. In short, you can't recall every memory at the same time. We only remember it when we need it. The third process is the retrieval process. This is when our brains bring a memory into our consciousness.

How Can Improving Your Memory Improve Your Life?

Improving your memory can improve your life in a number of ways. In a personal way, improving your memory can make it easier to recall names, birthdates, addresses, and other special information about the people you know and love. It can also be helpful even for a run to the grocery store. Imagine if you could actually remember what you went to the store to buy without needing to write it down. In a professional sense, having a better memory can help you in a number of ways. It can help you remember the names of key people for projects or even the names of new and important business contacts. It's impressive to business minded people when others can remember their name even if it's been a few days since they last spoke. It's also helpful for remembering important business facts. If you're in sales, then your prospects can be wowed during your initial meeting or during a follow up meeting when you are able to recall exactly which problem they told you about. If you're a student in a college (or really even just a student of life), improving your memory can mean learning more in a shorter amount of time. It could mean that your study time is decreased because you are better able to remember new information. It could mean that you don't have to study as hard for final exams because you can easily recall the information that you learned prior to that point.

Clearly, that was not an all-inclusive list on how your life can improve with a better memory. Although we all have things we need to remember, our lives are an individual piece of the world. So, how your life will be impacted by better memory will be unique to your life.

How the Brain and Your Memory Work

We've already discussed a little of how memory works using three main processes. Now, we will talk about the different types of memory and how it is organized by our brains. In 1968, Atkinson and Shiffrin gave the world a theory that explained the three main stages of memory.

Sensory memory is the earliest stage of memory. Information from our environment is held in our brain for a very short period of time. It could be as little time as half of a second for visual information. It could be as much as four seconds for things that we hear. With this basic type of memory, we do not remember everything. Even if you think about your first date,

4

you might remember the name of the wait staff but you probably won't remember the color of hair the lady had that sat at the next table. The pieces that you do remember during this time go on into the next form of memory.

Short term memory is the next form of memory. It is also known as your active memory. It is the information that you are conscious of during any period of time. Some people refer to it as the conscious mind. The sensory memories that we spoke about in the former paragraph generate information that is then stored as a short term memory. These pieces of information are stored in our mind for about 30 seconds. If we try to think about and recall this information, then it moves on to the third form of memory.

Long term memory is the next form. This is how your mind continuously stores pieces of information to recall at a later date. It's not information that we always think about, but we do think about it when we need it. If you know how to ride a bike, you most likely don't think about the motions involved in successfully doing it while you are doing the laundry. However, the minute you get on the bike then your body and your brain remember what you are supposed to do. It's not always easy to remember things. Even if a memory is hard to bring up, it's still stored in your long term memory. Some people refer to long term memory as the working memory.

It is not fully understood how our brains organize and store long term memories. However, researches have been able to show that our memories are stored in groups. Before we explain that in more detail, we'll give you an easy way to understand the concept. We've all had a moment in time that we've recalled a memory. Then, that memory reminded us of something else. Then, the second memory reminded us of a third memory. It could have been something small in the memory that pulled another memory to the surface of our awareness. That is the simple explanation of how our memories are organized into groups. The idea in this paragraph is an example of what researches refer to as the semantic network model.

The groups are referred to as clusters. It's where our brain associates things together. For instance, if you think of a glass then you might think of your favorite drink. Then, you might think of the place that you buy your favorite drink. That is a cluster. We also organize things by color. If you think of the word red, then you might think of a red shirt. The shirt might remind you of the pants you wear with the shirt.

How to Test Your Memory

There are many ways that you can test your memory. Since we live in an age of abundant technology, it's often easiest and most convenient to use an app or a program that is specifically used for testing your memory. We will talk more specifically about some of the apps that you can use to test and improve your memory at the end of this ebook. Those brain games will also help you improve your memory.

Many college websites have memory tests online as well. Using a reputable website (such as one associated with a well-known college) can give you peace of mind about your results. These are a form of self-testing, but they allow you to either try to memorize and recall information or they ask you questions and you apply a simple rating system. Then, you are able to score your test when you are finished.

Another method of testing involves self-testing. This is particularly good if you are a student and studying for a test. The idea is very simple and basic. You simply make up your own test questions. This can be done on paper by multiple choice or you can even make flash cards with the question on one side and the answer on the other. You can also use this technique of self-testing with a study buddy.

Of course, if you are worried that there may be something wrong with your memory then you can always speak with a psychologist, psychiatrist, or even your personal doctor to have your memory professionally tested. This is important as we get older. Many of us have trouble with remembering things as we get older. Some of that is simply part of the aging process, but it's also important to rule out any sort of problematic behaviour such as Alzheimer's disease and dementia.

When testing your memory for yourself, you need to understand your memory strengths and weaknesses. Since we are all individuals, it is important to realize that the way we remember things is also different. You may be really good at remembering numbers, but you may not be good at remembering names. Whereas, your sister may be great at names but she struggles to remember numbers.

It's also important to note that self-testing of any sort should not be used as a diagnostic tool. Again, if you are worried that there may be something wrong past needing to slightly enhance your ability to remember things, then you should visit with a professional about your testing options. A self-test or computerized app is simply a tool to give you a good idea of where you are with your abilities. It allows you to see progress as you enact some of the helpful tools and tricks you will find in this ebook.

Memory Improvement Methods

You are reading this ebook for one reason. You want to improve your memory. That's a great thing. You'll be able to recall information faster than you could before. The procedures below are some of the most popular ways to improve your memory. Choose the methods that seem most natural to you. You may find more than one method helpful and that's okay. It's great to find ways to improve your memory. You can even modify any of these methods in a manner that will work best for you.

The goal of this section is to act as a guide for you. If you enjoy music and other creative activities, then you might check out the methods that involve music and rhyming. If you tend to remember things by repetition, then you might want to check out flash cards. If you enjoy both flash cards and poetry, then you can integrate them and put your information in poetry form on the flash cards. It really is up to you. You should work to use as many of your senses as possible. That can result in faster learning and is known as multisensory learning.

Flash Cards

Flash cards can be made by the person who needs them or many types can be bought from a book store or a store that sells educational material. Index cards work great if you plan to make your own flash cards. Flash cards are great because they are portable. So, you can review your new information. Writing out the information will also help you remember it.

You can use flash cards to learn close to anything that you want. The goal is to keep the information short that is written on each card. Flash cards are ideal for math or scientific formulas, vocabulary words, definitions, dates, and even names. If you're a student, that's great news. You can use flash cards for practically any class.

Make sure that you prepare your flash cards early. In addition to writing out the information, you will give yourself more time to review it. This will help you remember the information. Keep your cards with you. This will remind you to review your information.

You should use both sides of the card. Write a word on one side of the card and the answer or definition of the other. This even works for mathematical formulas. You could write 'Operation of order' on one side. The other side would list 'PEMDAS' or the explanation of what each letter means.

Spend more time reviewing the terms that you can't remember versus spending it on common terms or things that you know. After all, the goal is to learn new information. You should shuffle the cards and review them in various orders. Remember that when you are tested on the new information that it won't necessarily be in the order that you reviewed it. You don't want your brain to only associate the information in one specific order.

Your flash cards don't just have to benefit you. They can also benefit your friends or classmates. You can each make a set that covers a different set of facts or information. Review your cards and then switch. You can also use them and quiz each other on a regular basis. You can even choose to make flash cards that cover the same information. However, you can each write a different fact about the idea that you are learning about.

Mnemonics

Mnemonics are memory devices that are helpful for retrieving information in your long term memory. This is especially helpful when you are learning new information that isn't really common to your life. That means that you don't have a knowledge base that will help you understand and remember the new information.

A mnemonic device can be a mental image, a visual picture, or something that you hear that can help you recall information. Here are some examples of common mnemonic devices that you most likely learned in school.

- Roy G. Biv is a name that reminds you of the color spectrum. It stands for red, orange, yellow, green, blue, indigo, and violet. The name is an acronym.
- In English, you learned about I before E except after C unless ending in "A" like neighbor and weigh. That is an example of a rhyming mnemonic.
- When you took music in school, you learned the basics of reading music. Your teacher told you that **every good boy does fine**. The first letter of each sentence is an acrostic which is a form of mnemonic device that we will soon discuss. The first letter of each word of the sentence represents a line on the staff.

The great thing about mnemonics is that you can make them fit you. If you can't remember Roy G. Biv, you could make up a sentence like is commonly used to teach basic music notes.

You can make up your very own mnemonics or even look them up online. There are mnemonic websites available about a wide variety of subjects. Below, we will look at a few common mnemonic devices in closer detail.

Acronyms

We use acronyms every day in our lives. In some cases, acronyms make up an actual word (or at least something we can pronounce). Sometimes, they don't. NASA is an acronym that stands for National Aeronautics and Space Administration. Although, NASA isn't an actual word, the organization behind the acronym is more commonly known as the acronym as opposed to the actual organizational name.

An acronym that doesn't make a word or something easy to pronounce is still an acronym. When you have an acronym that's made up of a set of letters like this, then you have the definition of an actual acronym. This is a great way to remember a list of items. Instead of memorizing the entire list, you can simply choose to remember the first letter of each item. If you meet Bob, Sue, Ray, Debra, and Chris then you might choose to just remember BSRDC instead of each person's name. That would be a handy way to remember the people that you need to purchase Christmas gifts for during the holiday season.

Acrostics

An acrostic is a fun way to remember new information. If you have a list of words that you want to remember, take the first letter of each word and use those letters to make a new word.

You could also take the letters and make a new sentence. Acrostics are very close to acronyms. An acronym is, of course, an abbreviation that stands for a longer word or set of words. An acrostic can be very short like an acronym as well. The goal of making an acrostic is to make sure that it is something memorable for you.

If you met Deputy Officer John Odd, then you would use the letters D, O, J, and O. You could make a word (dojo). You could use it as a partial acronym (D.O.J. for Department of Justice). You could even come up with a sentence that will help you remember his position and name using only those letters we previously listed.

Acrostics can be difficult to learn. They do get easier with practice. It's important to remember that the information you use should make sense to you or be memorable to you. Many people try to make their acrostic match the event or time that they are trying to remember. It's okay if yours doesn't match. What matters is that you are able to use the technique in a way that can help you remember the needed information. Sometimes, acrostics can be incredibly easy. If you have items that can be easily grouped, it makes it simple to use. If you meet Bryan, Jacob, and Patrick for a sales meeting then you can remember PB&J just like the sandwich! Acrostics are also easy if you enjoy silly sentences. You can take the first letter of each item you want to remember and write a silly sentence. If you want to remember zebras, elephants, and bears then you could write a sentence such as: zombies eat brains. It's silly and memorable.

Chunking

Chunking is one of the world's oldest ways to remember information. You take the final outcome of what you are trying to learn and break it down into smaller pieces. This works best if the information that you need to learn and then later remember doesn't need to be recalled in any particular order. You may already do this without recognizing that it has a name. For instance, if someone gives you their new phone number then you might find yourself breaking the numbers up into smaller groups. Perhaps you remember it by reciting it either two or three numbers at a time. Maybe you recite the area code, pause, first three digits, pause, and then say the last four digits. This is chunking. Many people do it when they are spelling words as well. They break a large, difficult to remember word into smaller groups of letters.

It is helpful to try and group the information in your brain in helpful ways. If you have a grocery list that lists celery, apples, milk, lettuce, and cheese then you might do better to start by saying two vegetables, two dairy products, and one fruit. Then, you can reorganize your list (even if it is just in your head) to match the more organized information. This is particularly helpful if your list is no longer than nine items. Studies have shown that our short term memory most effectively holds and recalls lists of no more than nine items.

Loci Method: The Memory Palace

The Loci Method is also known as the memory palace method. If you've ever read or watched Silence of the Lambs, then you have a pretty good understanding of the idea behind the Loci Method. In Silence of the Lambs, Dr. Lecter is incarcerated and often has his books and other personal belongings confiscated. However, it doesn't seem to bother him. In the movie (spoiler alert), he reveals how his childhood tutor had taught him how to memorize information. He designed a palace in his mind and stored his information inside. Your memory palace can be as elaborate or as simple as you would like to make it. It's fantastic memory technique and it's easy to learn.

The Loci Method was developed more than 2000 years ago. It was used by ancient Greeks and Romans to enable them to deliver long speeches. During those days, delivering a speech by memory was a highly prized and respected ability. Being able to repeat this process and give speeches or sales presentations without referring to a set of notes is very impressive.

This method is a visual walk through of your information. You store each piece of information inside of your memory palace. Clearly, since you want to remember this information in a certain order then you should start from the beginning of your palace. Items without your introduction should be stored in the walk way or foyer of your memory palace. You can use anything you would like in your mind to visually associate the ideas and remind yourself of what you need to say. You can imagine other things in that area as well. It's your memory palace. You can use each thing that you "decorate" your memory palace with as a peg or a hook for the new information. You can make it realistic or you can make it silly. It's really whatever will help you best remember the information.

When you are ready to recall the information, simply walk through your memory palace while speaking. It is important that you practice this technique on a regular basis. You don't want to be caught in a moment where you've forgotten something. Mentally walk through your palace on a regular basis in order to keep the associations in the forefront of your mind.

Rhymes

Although there is generally only one way that we think about rhyming, you can actually use this in two ways. You can simply make up a rhyme about what you want to memorize or you can use it in the form of a mnemonic device. Remember, we discussed earlier that a mnemonic device can be something audible or it can be something that gives you a visual image. When used as a rhyme, it can both be audible and give you a distinct mental image.

For instance, if you met a new potential business contact named Sue then you could make a rhyme. It doesn't matter if it is true or not. The goal is to associate Sue with something that sticks in your mind. Your rhyme might look something like this:

I met Sue and she wore one red shoe.

That is both a simple rhyme and something that gives you a mental image. Of course, it would be helpful if she wore red shoes when you first met her. However, it still works as an excellent mental image.

There are rhymes that you learned in school that perfectly illustrate how to use this type of mnemonic device. Remember I before E except after C? That's a perfect example. So is the rhyme about which months have 31 days and which months have 30 days.

It's important to note that rhymes won't be helpful in all forms of new information. It's important that you try to keep this mnemonic device simple. You don't want to find yourself frustrated and feel as if you are unable to learn new information.

Music

Music is a great way to learn. In fact, it's one of the earliest ways we learn. In kindergarten or even before kindergarten you learned your ABCs by song. You might have learned to count to ten by singing a song such as Ants Go Marching On or about the ten little bears jumping on the bed. The rhythm and rhyme associated in music helps our brain grasp new information. You can use a song or write a short song that is filled with the information that you're trying to remember. If you've ever had a day where you couldn't get a certain song out of your head, then you understand the power of catchy music.

If you enjoy writing poetry, then you could take music that you already are familiar with and write a parody of it. Weird Al is an excellent example of parody writing. You can do the same thing and use information that you want to learn.

Alliteration

You can also use alliteration as a memory tool. The key to alliteration is that you choose words that sound alike that you can associate together. Stem and stun are alliterations because they both contain the same beginning sounds. You can do the same thing with vowel sounds as well. If you have a long list to remember, you can reorganize it into sections that sound alike in some way.

Jokes

Jokes are a great way to remember information. They can take be a silly rhyme or it can even be a pun. There are lots of clever jokes on the Internet about a wide variety of subjects. In addition to helping you retain information, you'll also have something funny to tell your family or friends at a later time in order to show them your new knowledge. Here's an example of a joke that would help you remember who and whom:

Knock knock
Who's there?
To.
To who?
No, to whom.

Visual Images and Association

Visual images can be something that you see only in your head or something that you can put into physical action. If you were taught how to remember which months have 31 days using the knuckles of your hands, then you were taught a visual association mnemonic device. You can use whatever sort of visual image or physical action that helps you remember the new information.

There are three quite common ways to use visual imagery as a mnemonic device. The first common method is the keyword method. It's really effective if you need to memorize definitions or vocabulary words. Many people use it when they are learning a new language. The goal is to take two pieces of information and link them together. In short, you want to associate the ideas. Take the sound of at least one of the concepts. Then, find a mental or physical image that you can associate with it. If you were trying to learn more about phonetics, you could picture someone talking on the phone. After all, the idea is that we use phonetics to communicate the sound that letters make (and turn them into words to tell others).

The second common visual association mnemonic is the link method. This is perfect if you need to memorize lists. It is called the link method because it connects ideas together much like the links of a fence. It works well because so many of us have the ability to recall imagery. First, visualize a funny or memorable image that represents the type of list that you want to make. It can be helpful if you incorporate the first thing on your list into your image. Next, incorporate a silly or memorable visual of the second item on your list that is somehow associated with the first item. Continue this process until you've visually linked every item on your list. As long as you can keep your mental images clear, then you will have no problem remembering your list. Remember to start with one item for a visual image. Then you can do another image with two items. If you have three items, then you take the second and the third item to make a visual image. The process gets easier as you practice it.

The peg system is the third most common visual mnemonic that people use. It is most commonly used by those who must remember their listed information in a particular order. This method works well because we take the new information and associate it with information that we already know. The idea of a peg is simply a mental hook that you will use to hold the new information. One of the easiest ways to learn to do this is to incorporate a number and rhyme system. Essentially, each peg that will help you recall the new information will rhyme with a number. Here's a written example:

1 – sun
2 – shoe
3 – tree
4 – door
5 – hive

Those will be your pegs. Now, you will use visualization. The first thing to be recalled should be pictured with the sun involved. It's okay if your image is a bit silly. You go through the entire list incorporating the rhyming word with your required information. If you go above 20 or if you have a number that is hard to rhyme, you can pick out your own images to act as pegs. Instead of numbers, you could use the alphabet.

There are other ways to visualize and associate information. You can make your own or you can look online for ideas. You can even use visualization and association with the sounds that words make. Have you ever heard a word and thought it was something totally different than what it was based off of the sound? Your brain tried to associate it with something that it visualized. That happened most likely based off of sound. You can do the same thing but make the visualization for your benefit. You can also just break down certain parts of the word to help you remember. The word maintenance is a good example. Many people have a hard time remembering whether it is spelled with an e or an a after the t. You can solve this for yourself by visualizing: main10ance. The number 10 is spelled with an e in the middle.

Outlining

Many people find outlining new information very beneficial for memorization and recall. This is an excellent way to organize information that you're reading or that you've heard during a lecture. Outlining can be highly structured and involve the use of Roman numerals or the alphabet. You can also make your own outline that is more informally structured. The basic outline structure looks similar to this:

I. Main Topic
A. Sub-topic
1. Point about sub-topic.
2. Point about sub-topic.
3. Point about sub-topic.

B. Sub-topic

II. Another Main Topic
A. Sub-topic
1. Point about sub-topic.
2. Point about sub-topic.
3. Point about sub-topic.

You would keep going until you've reached the end. The idea is to list only the most important or even the most interesting information about the topic. You can use an outline to study or even to put together a paper. An outline can be very handy. You can even use mind-mapping software on your computer to construct an outline. It's not nearly as formal as the example provided above, but it gives you a great opportunity to make sure you list every part of your paper or information that you should cover.

Even if you don't have access to a computer, you can still use a mind-map. You can use plain paper and a writing utensil. In school, you might have learned this as brain storming. You put your main idea or topic in the middle of the page. Then, you write your sub-topics around it. Sometimes, people circle those and use a line to point it back from the topic. Each sub-topic may also have lines connected to other bubbles that hold a key word or a very short phrase about it. The idea is to stimulate your brain to remember certain information associated with the information that is circled.

Repetition

Repetition can be used by itself or with any of the other tools that are listed in this ebook. You want to repeat new information in order to keep it fresh in your mind or to make sure that you will remember it. It can be that you put the information into action. For instance, if you meet a new colleague named Daniel and you want to make sure that you remember his name, then you should make sure and repeat his name in a natural manner during your conversation. It could be as simple as saying the following sentences (within the proper context):

Hi, Daniel. It's nice to meet you.

So, Daniel how are you enjoying your new responsibilities?

Where did you go to college, Daniel?

Using a naturally repetitive way to insert a name will help your brain associate the person's face to the name.

Of course, repetition isn't always that easy and it often isn't seen as a fun task. It is a necessity that we all work with in order to retain and later recall information. This is particularly important for those who give any sort of presentation. Make sure that you practice your presentation in order for it to be your best.

Teaching Others

Teaching others is a great way to solidify what you've learned. If you don't have the opportunity to teach a class, you can still do this exercise to show that you've learned the information. The goal is to take the information and, no matter the subject matter, break it down in a way that an average person can understand.

You should be able to teach at least the basic concepts of what you've learned to an average child. That means that you eliminate industry slang and learn to discuss new concepts in a way that anyone can understand. When you do this, you must be able to teach it in a way that does not seem patronizing to others.

Public Speaking

If there is a subject that you are particularly enthusiastic about, you can find opportunities to engage in public speaking. We aren't necessarily talking about paid gigs. Often, public speaking on a local level is something that you simple do as volunteer. You can volunteer to speak to teenagers, speak at library events, or even join organizations such as Toastmasters. You will gain great experience and more confidence as you talk with others. You'll also get feedback on how to better teach or talk about your chosen topic.

Writing

Writing is another excellent way to reinforce new concepts. In class, you may be assigned an essay. Even if you don't necessarily enjoy writing, you should understand the educational value that exists. Writing out information in your own words will help you retain what you've learned.

If you enjoy writing, you have opportunities to write about your knowledge. You can start a blog that is dedicated to your subject matter. This is particularly helpful if you truly are interested in what you are learning. It can even be a broad subject such as science. You could write about the information in a way that young students or their parents could understand. You could include experiments or practical ways to teach the new information. You can look up magazines or websites that accept submissions about the subject matter. Make sure that you follow their instructions for consideration. This is a great way that you can write about the material and in some cases you may even make money.

Additional Learning Methods

Bed time recital is another learning method that is highly prized. It is thought to be so effective because we are in a relaxed state of mind at the time that we are getting ready for bed. The mind will work to process and retain the information for later recall while you are sleeping.

Believe it or not, another effective learning method is to just not try so hard to remember. We've all had that moment when we've had a word at the tip of our tongue that we simply can't remember. Then, when we stop trying so hard, we suddenly remember it. Although this clearly won't be effective at a time that you must have the information immediately, it is still a great way to remember new information.

You can learn new information by taking up new past times that help you increase your focus and concentration. You can start doing crossword puzzles or even begin to play certain types of board games that involve critical thinking skills. Learning to concentrate will help your brain learn to retain new information.

Do an Internet search on effective ways to learn about your intended subject matter. You will find websites, games, and learning methods devoted to it. This is a great way to find specific ways to learn.

How to Take Effective Notes

Many people get overwhelmed when they try to take notes. They try to write down everything that is being said or they write down information from a chapter that ends up being non-essential. Learning to take effective notes can take some practice. However, note taking is a great study skill. It gives you material to review (repetition). Many people also learn faster when they write the information down. Here are some tips on how to take effective notes:

Dedicate a notebook or folder to each individual subject that you may use to store your notes. It can be confusing and frustrating to put all of your notes on different subjects into one folder or notebook. Make it easy to find what you need by separating out your subject matter notes.

If you're using a textbook, look at the review questions or end of chapter questions before you read the chapter or attend class. Those questions can give you a good idea of what is important in each chapter. That is the information that may be on the test. However, other information may be on the test as well. Look at the objectives and section summaries in order to know what may be covered as well. Looking for the answers of the questions or the information in the summaries can help you find the appropriate information that belongs inside of your notes.

Practice active listening in your course lectures. You want to make sure that you are able to take notes on the most important information that is presented by your instructor. Listen for key phrases and watch for key actions that can help you decide if the information they are discussing may appear on a test. Key phrases can include "You'll see this on a test" or "You may see this on a quiz" are important and obvious ways to tell you what to study.

If your instructor writes something on the board, then you should put it in your notes. First, writing it for yourself will help the information stick in your brain. Second, if an instructor finds it important enough to take the time to write it out for you, then they may put it on a test. Instructors often take the time to emphasis important pieces of information.

Label your notes. You can choose whatever labelling method works best for you. You can label it by subject and by date. If your information is over a specific chapter, then you may want to include the chapter title as well. This will help you when it's time to study for mid-term and final tests.

Health and Exercise Benefits on Memory

Health and exercise are highly beneficial to your memory. Much like the majority of your body, your brain has the ability to regenerate certain types of material. The hippocampus is the memory center of your brain. Having an active and healthy lifestyle will help your hippocampus grow new cells.

It's important that you cut as many toxins out of your life as possible. This can include exposure to chemicals and even a poor diet. Lack of sleep and too much stress are also quite toxic to us in many ways. In order to support a healthy brain, you must be willing to engage in healthy behaviour patterns.

Here are seven ways that you can help your brain be at its best even as you age.

1. Eat the right foods to support your brain. We're told to feed our babies certain types of fatty foods in order to help the development of their brains. We are even given time frames on when the brain stops growing. However, just because it stops growing in size doesn't mean that it stops renewing itself. The foods you choose play a very important role in how your brain functions. Make sure that you get plenty of fresh vegetables and the right amount of the good fats. Minimize your sugar and grain carbohydrate intake. Healthy fats include omega 3 fats such as krill or fish oil. Coconut oil is believed to help minimize the risk of degenerative neurological disorders.

2. Make sure that you get enough exercise. While we know that changes are made to what experts consider

as the right amount exercise, it is still important that you are exercising. If you are new to exercising, work your way up to the appropriate time. It's also important that you talk with your doctor about any exercise program that you decide to implement. Exercise encourages your brain to work at its best level. It can strengthen your nerve cells and encourage them to reproduce. It also protects the nerves of your brain against damage. During exercise, your brain releases proteins that encourage your brain to continue to repair itself. People that exercise on a regular basis help their brain grow the hippocampus.

3. Multitasking isn't your friend. Although our work environments and our constant state of busy living often demand that we do more than one thing at once, multitasking isn't good for your brain. Multitasking can slow you down and cause you to forget what you should be doing or how you should do it. Instead, you should practice mindfulness. Focusing on the task at hand will help you fully learn and reinforce the involved concepts.

4. Get enough sleep. Sleep is another subject that experts seem to change their opinion about on a regular basis. However, you should make sure that you're getting enough sleep. In general, experts currently recommend around seven hours per sleep each night for adults. A recent study shows that missing four hours of sleep has the same effect on your brain and your ability to focus to the effect of if you had decided to drink an entire six pack of beer. Sleep can enhance your memory. Loss of sleep can affect your brain's ability to grow.

5. Exercise your brain. Make sure that you challenge your brain. New information will help keep your brain from

deteriorating. Something as simple as playing brain games for 20 minutes can help your brain grow.

6. Learn something new. After all, the goal of this ebook is to help you learn more and remember it better. The only way to truly learn the concepts in this book is to apply them. Make it a habit to learn something new. You condition your brain and make it easier to recall information using the tools above by making the use of them a habit. The skill that you choose can be something that you're interested in. It doesn't have to be something that requires you to spend hours studying. In fact, keeping it fun and interesting will help you increase the desire to learn. If you enjoy gardening, then learn something new about gardening or purchase a new plant that requires a different type of cultivation than you currently use in your garden.

7. Learn to use mnemonic devices. Although they can be tricky to learn, they can also be fun and very helpful. Since there is more than one type of mnemonic device, you can choose one that works best for your learning style. One of the easiest types of mnemonic devices includes an acronym. Take a small task that you can turn into an actual word. For instance if you needed to carry out stinky trash, you could turn it into COST.

In addition to keeping your brain healthy, you should also keep your digestive system healthy. Your digestive system is almost like a second brain. It sends information to your brain through the vagus nerve. There is a very close connection to your brain health and the health of your digestive system. Your digestive tract produces neurons (including serotonin) which can cause mood disturbances. Mood disturbances can make it harder to learn. Make sure that you keep your gut healthy by avoiding large quantities of sugar and by taking probiotics.

Resources You Can Use

As we briefly discussed earlier in this ebook, there are apps and online websites that can help you increase your cognitive abilities. This is done by playing brain games for at least 20 minutes each day. In this section we will discuss a few of the options that are available online or in app form. This is not every available option. You can look around and find your own favorites!

Luminosity is a website that takes science and memory games and makes them fun. They take cognitive tasks and turn them into games that can help you strengthen your ability to learn and retain new information. You get tests and a personal brain trainer. It's available online and also has an app for all major smart phone operating systems. You can also get an email to remind you to do your brain training.

Dual N back training isn't limited to just one website. There are several websites and apps that offer this feature. Dual N back training is used to increase your IQ and better your memory. You participate in this training for around 20 minutes a day for about 20 days to see maximum results. There are free and paid apps available for use.

Quizlet does more than just help you train your brain. You can create flash cards and use other study tools. The amazing thing about this website is that it was actually created by a high school student. There are currently more than 40 million study sets available for public use. They have a free and paid membership. You can create your own set of flash cards and even ad graphics. They also have tests that are rather fun!

Quizlet offers an audio option for more than 18 languages. They even have an app for Apple and Android products.

NeuroNation is a website that offers free brain games. It has easy games that help you enhance your ability to remember and recite new information. According to their website, you only need to play their games for ten minutes each day. They measure your cognitive function using five distinct categories. During each training session, you will play games that cover each category. One of the unique features of this website is the ability to issue challenges to your friends and family.

Improving your memory is a great and effective way to improve your life. Through the techniques and resources outlined in this book, you have everything you need to get started. Remember, practice makes perfect. You won't achieve what you want if you don't practice. So use this book as a resource to look back on and continue to improve your memory each and everyday!

A Free Gift

I want to say Thank You for buying my book so I put together a free gift for you!

Nutrients and Smart Drugs That Help Memory

This gift is the perfect complement to this book so just vist the link below to get access.

http://www.mylanderpages.com/freegifts/MentalMastery

Thanks!

Jason

Disclaimer and Terms of Use: Effort has been made to ensure that the information in this book is accurate and complete, however, the author and the publisher do not warrant the accuracy of the information, text and graphics contained within the book due to the rapidly changing nature of science, research, known and unknown facts and internet. The Author and the publisher do not hold any responsibility for errors, omissions or contrary interpretation of the subject matter herein. This book is presented solely for motivational and informational purposes only.

www.ingramcontent.com/pod-product-compliance
Lightning Source LLC
Chambersburg PA
CBHW070751180526
45168CB00004B/1580